Made in United States
Orlando, FL
07 May 2022

17634082R00061